joie de vivre

The Collected Poems of

Roseanna Frechette

Joie de Vivre

© 2025, Roseanna Frechette

Books may be purchased in quantity and/or special sales by contacting the author.

Roseanna Frechette

roseanna.frechette@gmail.com

First Paperback Edition, 2025

ISBN: 979-8-218-72013-1
Library of Congress Control Number: 2025916092

Cover Photo: Mary Heins

Cover Design: Brice Maiurro

Author Image: Pat James

Edited by: Jerry Smaldone, Carolyn Reed, Brice Maiurro

Passion Press, Denver CO
Printed in the United States

Praise for *Joie de Vivre*

"There is undeniable magic in this remarkable collection of poetry. Roseanna Frechette's voice translates with grace and honesty the heights and depths of the vulnerable soul as it seeks out the joy of life. This collection is a joy itself and worth reading again and again."

—Carolyn Reed
Author of *Maze Bright*
Founding Member of Denver Union of Street Poets

"I loooove this book. *Love* it! So strong, great flow. A book that someone will pick up many, many times, to be reminded of the beautiful struggle life is. There is a vulnerable yet fierce personal quality that appeals to me and will attract many others. Emotions are borne, but in a most artistic way. It is a victory for the individual that is all of us. Frechette's poetic qualities stand out, complex yet understandable.

In the dense corridors of emotion, in this poet's cerebral machinations, in the visions of the natural world, there is an openness, a vulnerability, a real, live person who shyly lets you peek into her soul, her mind, and still yells from the mountain top her own wild truth. What a combination! As I repeatedly go through the poems, I'm blown away by the great lines and insights, the strings of interrelated impressions and the raw depth of emotions. No should's, but Roseanna should be very proud of this work. It really is her."

—Jerry Smaldone
Author of *Fatto a Mano* & *All Flesh Shall See It Together*

"In Roseanna Frechette's collection of poems, spanning decades of her life, her poetry seemingly jumps off the page and into the hearts and minds of its readers. The same electricity that she has brought to Denver's art community and beyond is captured like lightning in a bottle in the vibrant spirit present in these poems. These poems are a deep yogic breath inward and out, as quiet as they are loud, energized and ready to confront hard truths and also to invite you in to share in beautiful moments."

—Brice Maiurro
Editor-in-Chief of *South Broadway Press*

"Roseanna Frechette invites the reader to peer through her lens as she shifts her gaze from Colorado landscapes and urban settings to broader contemplations. Her refusal to romanticize combines with a rare tenderness that explores the sometimes-brutal world from an angle of deep joy."

—Leah Rogin
Author of *Burying Norma Jeane*

"Frechette hails from a French-Canadian family resettled in Northwest Indiana...but that is mere historicity. The lady can WRITE and *that* she does with a broad brush from a Kerouac-infused drive, mixed with a little Anaïs Nin perspective. Follow Roseanna as she takes the reader on a journey from a youth in the Midwest to bohemian Denver and further out to the wilderness of Colorado. She takes the reader "down to the skin" and you can feel the rock formations, the wildlife, and the rarified air of the mountain passes. There are many Zen moments in this book from feeling the "sleet in your face" to the "hail that soon comes." Experience her *Joie de Vivre*.

—Guillermo Lazo
Editor, *Rocky Mountain Arsenal of the Arts*

Introduction
Words From the Author

This retrospective collection has been a long time coming, and I thank all the poetry-loving people that have encouraged me to bring it about. With particular gratitude to my husband Tom for building me a stellar writing studio in which to happily complete the work.

I didn't choose the title of this book. It chose me. The French phrase "Joie de Vivre," is directly translated as "Joy of Life," usually thought of as happiness found through energetic enthusiasm for living. Although I experience this, my interpretation of the phrase is not necessarily about happiness. More so, it's about accepting all aspects of life (even the difficult ones) with a vibrant spirit. My life includes inherent joy that comes when I genuinely embrace it all.

Joie de Vivre is a French-Canadian legacy, passed on to me most certainly by my Quebecoise mother who immigrated to the U.S. while in her 20s. My father, a reputable musician from the Chicago/Kankakee area and also of French-Canadian descent, further secured that legacy. The spirit of my parents, Aline Vezina and Frigon Frechette, gratefully continues to inspire me.

Born in the U.S Midwest, I relocated to Colorado at the age of 19. In decades to follow, Denver's bohemian underground became, for me, the perfect place in which to embrace a creative life.

Although I now reside in Colorado's mountain town of Salida, my heart and soul continue in the bohemian community of our world. Which is to say, among those that live for, and through, art~ *and* are willing to live an unconventional lifestyle in order to do so.

It is to this way of living that I dedicate my book. For I truly believe that expressing oneself through art (of any kind), while also embracing that journey, is finding a doorway to one's soul.

Salut~

TABLE OF CONTENTS

Part One: Joie *(Joy)*
Breaking Open

Part Two: de *(of)*
Breaking Through

Part Three: Vivre *(Life)*
Breaking Free

joie de vivre

Roseanna Frechette

PASSION PRESS
DENVER CO USA

Part One: Joie *(Joy)*
Breaking Open

A blank page
is like an open sky,
nothing
to be feared.

Colorado Woman Song

1.

Raven eats squirrel
by the side of the road
I ride over blue mesa
the heart of me passing
from blue to lush green
like the gourd song
of Telluride
echoing back from the distance
again, Colorado, your landscape
has softened sharp edges
of something so hard to live with.
I find it quite smooth now, it's full
and it's flowing.
The water is aquamarine, sun-streaked
spirit of poetry pilgrim
en route home and crossing these
rainbow-like bridges she built
in a lifetime of learning that history
is something we make for ourselves.

2.

South on 285 the cattle are watching the river flow.
What else have they got to do?
I honk at them, smile and wave, thinking:
"Colorado cattle—mellow beasts with good karma."

3.
Colorado, I came to you seeking
a path for my spirit to soar on.
A wounded young woman-child, curious, hopeful.
You opened up color-filled skyfulls and vistas,
stark, stunning ranges of snowy peaks, wildflowers,
waterfalls, endless these acres of
trees, trees, trees, trees.

4.
I am of sky.
I run with the clouds.
I am the river breathing in color blue/grey.
Singing softly of pink smoke reflections.
I am the rhythm of rock earth.
It gives me life.

Between Meaning

Seasons change and I long to go back
to a place that has never existed.
In my mind, I must try to go back
like running in dream with eyes closed
I sense true destination that I never see.
It isn't there.
A whirlpool with heart, but no heartbeat.
A treehouse that holds comfort, empty space.

When seasons change, I become like a traveler
going nowhere.
I slip between meaning of
wine coolers and whiskey heat.
I wish to be unspent youth,
too secure in what I don't know yet.
    I want to go back.
    I want to go back.

There's a memory I have: smell of dead leaves.
Big pile of burnt orange, brown, gold,
amber, crimson.
My friends bury me there on Boulevard.
Boogie man chases us home.
  Sound of steak frying, french fries and voices,
    a family/a meal/a milk pitcher full.

Running, I'm running in dream.
I cannot see through blizzard,
big snowflakes that never stop falling.
A Christmas tree: red green white blue lights
mix into the color of color.

It's drawing me in
just to wonder why we take it down
leaving place that doesn't exist where it was.

Seasons change and I want to go back.
Desperate drivenness I never speak of
lands me in a deluge of rainstorms
that promise me what?

I can't know as I try to go back
every time crocus earth opens.
White rose unfolding a lifetime of seasons I long for,
to go back, to a place that I know is there,
even though it never really existed. At all.

Narcissus Echo

17th Avenue coffee shop gaze
sipping double espresso
sun streak of windowpane.
Her face appears in the glass
half in light
half in shadow
mysterious green-eyed face floating.
And she who can never find
beauty enough in herself
is amazed at the beauty of woman she sees
half like hand-colored photograph
half black and white then dissolving abstract
gold hoop earring glint sparks
as her trademark.
> *Remembers the time she was shown*
> *an x-ray of her skull and neck bones*
> *that hoop earring was there...*

As she writes sun gone down
glass etched face disappears
when she looks for it
she sees black hole with hoop earrings.
Beyond 17th
someone's lawn/white sports car
parked with black trees half bare
twist of leaves falling down
leaves of golden and brown.
> *Remembers the time she was shown*
> *a photo of her face*
> *she admired, not knowing*
> *such beauty could belong to her...*

Narcissus echo
cool pleasure
the art form of seeing one's own face abstract.
Narcissus echo
cool pleasure
the art form of finding one's own face in glass.

Out Into Forever

The black sky had that soft spring storm power... the sort of power that says: This is what you need right now... trust... change is on its way... change is what you love.

The woman was resting on her maroon velvet love seat, staring into an energy of nothing. Sweet tears developed from a most tender spot where emotion becomes saline, like sea water, connected to the next ocean wave. A tear-infused wave, soft as nothing. Was rolling itself out. Out into forever.

Hope

Blue eyes
long to see moon
balanced on
point of one star.

Calloused
the fingertips ache
to feel pink
clouds roll forward more.

On horizons
ablazen
thresholds stand renewed.

Mountain Writing Itself

Human words cannot save this
as rivers of raindrops, like tears,
travel ridges back up to red sky.

Breath of wind in my trees
singing blues/wild heart pulsing
black rock unconsidered.

Still, Heavy
I Scream.

Caving into blue/black
no one finds me.
I gather my flocks and my herds
into this time *this time* THIS
TIME may be *not safe*.

We stop in our tracks.

Spring Snow

Cool wet snowflakes
of mountain seasons past
melt across my mind.

Between These Walls

Something screams inside my ear
long before ringing has begun.
"Stop" I shout… then wait
and pause while muted voice of me unheard
joins clang of sound emergent,
sudden ringing, all too clear.
Right bells resound bright loud
from strange Cathedral.
Am I blessed?

Narrow passage beckons me
from yesterday but not the same.
Grand hallway spirals deep inside
like echo, ocean shell.

I want to know what job awaits me
in this moment ringing out.
What task. What undone effort.
What odd match with unmet mate.

Pant and scramble for a handhold,
shimmy tight between these walls.
Velvet press of hope unknown
closing in against my skin,
like great spiraling warm hallway,
smell of cinnamon and beige.
I am safe in narrow passage.
Need no mate. I am safe.

Scramble, shimmy, scramble,
shimmy through tight corridor of grace.
Between these walls of soft unknowing
comes the sound of I Am Safe.

Velvet press against my skin,
muted hope as yet unvoiced,
hears itself between these walls,
announcing passage, gently paced.
Chimes are singing, ringing softly,
toning, chiming, sounding out.
Radiant as bright Cathedral.
I am blessed. I Am Safe.

Eldorado Night Sky

Sending silent howls
up to the stars,
breathing invisible love
for an absent moon,
holding, holding, holding on
to a nameless thing
I was abandoned here to do.

And if you sit in darkness long enough
a wise old night may speak to you.
The stars keep arriving as they should,
bring not one promise only spark.

Holding, holding, holding on
to the hope of stars is futile.

As tall tree branches whisper
in a lonely naked voice,
no longer holding crimson leaves,
instead catch single falling stars.

First Sonnet

Oh love I cannot write you now.
Blue mystery face
glows only in his darkness.
Recede charred wick
from broken lantern,
burn no more.
See nothing clearer:
placid heart of lake bereavement.

Bright sky will rain for all tomorrow.
Soft rinse of wishes spoken free.

Stand still.
Your ground is breaking open.
Dark well of ink.
My pen just broke.

Tumbleweed

As I watch friends roll away on road trips, some planning to return, some not sure if they will I find it strangely comforting when a massive tumbleweed crosses my path on a busy city street, mid-week, mid-day... today.

Change asks...

Change asks for a sacrifice always.
And I am like a snake with phantom skin,
not yet realized that last inch of scaly stuff
is still hanging on the
chain link fence
of a past to which I belong
no more.

> Let me be the revolution.
> Let me be self-respect.
> Let me be non-violence.
> Let me be not afraid.
> Let me be creative.
> Let me be spirited.
> Let me be responsible.
> Let
> Me
> Be
> Change~.

Tightwire

For tightrope artist Philippe Petit who dared break civic law when he crossed New York's Twin Towers in 1974.

I've walked some fine line
like the man that imprinted himself
in my brain long ago
when young girl that I was could not stop
staring: TV screen, big news, a tiny man
clad in black slacks, ballet slippers
moving across air, against wind, absurdly high up
on a wire strung between two twin towers.

Even his name would remain in my brain
like a poem I've recited again and again
and so simply: Philippe Petit
must have been
quite acutely aware of one hard crash
velocity, asphalt,
mistakes one can never take back.
Not holding the breath
and not breathing too big
just aware of the place where a body
decides to stay safe
even though
it could flatten
set soul wild and free
when gold pot of ether and
tar pit of gravity meet.

I believe Monsieur Philippe Petit
may have sprinkled his balancing pole
with a weightlessness, poetry dust,
just before he broke civic law
tower to tower.

It was no small feat
that relied on a steady heartbeat
not to topple itself.

There's a poetry walking the tightwire.
It can keep the mob that is watching in darkness awake.

Even
when
we
cannot
write
it
down.

Water/Time/Rock
Colorado River, Grand Canyon, 1998

When going down to the core
marking time in rock you must
refuse to wear shoes or clothes
take yourself down to the skin
put your foot there and follow with
all of your bare skin, your soul
you of we
we of water
clear essence
we made to flow now
out of sync
with the dictates
of intellect (intellect maybe is
not quite the greatest
of human assets).

In my mind
take me down with my body
to rhythm
that started before I was born then
the first time my heart beat
skin muscle and bones
brain cells, blood stream all
wrapped around heartbeat
of spirit
that started with water
a long time ago
I don't even know when
but I feel I do when
I let the wave roll free

let water come through
as if this is all new
marking time in rock down to the core.

September Draw

Wind soft in these leaves.
I await a fourth sunrise today.
Two jet streams intersect
in a cotton-white X,
swarm of hummingbirds fly high,
one Lazuli Bunting flits by
cap bright blue as yr eyes.

And a cold tired fly
trances near me
as if to show:
some things eventually slow down,
then die
while the X overhead tips itself
gradually,
in slow motion,
from straight up
to right-tilting angle.
Soon it will flatten, dissolve.
But not before sending white light
through bright green spray of leaves
swaying off dark tree bark.

Many things will appear,
disappear on this day.
Save the Love.
Summer's gone.
It has changed us forever.

Shout of Sun appears fourth time today
like Great Trickster.

Shape Shifters aware:
free horizons are things we dream up
and then follow.

I love noiseless sound of this place
like the sound of my heart
beating toward you.

Crisis

Understand
the choice is not
to be trapped
in a box
no way to crawl out.

We discover
the lid
can be lifted
blown off
torn apart.

Meeting more
we never knew.

Joie de Vivre

Me, eating frosted cupcakes.
Me, skipping down the driveway.
Me, meditating solo... on a white sand beach.
Or watching bright light cool of June's strawberry moon,
at midnight and beyond.
Me knowing tiny gold finch pair, that landed
on the olive tree,
is only passing through.
Or seeing one blue heron, as it rests, on one leg,
beside a still city lake.
Or crying when someone I love is moving far away.

Me touring the world,
from Eiffel Tower in Paris
to Cajun Shrimp in New Orleans,
sometimes only in my dreams.

Does not mean for sure,
that what you see,
is what becomes of me.

We do what we do which seems so often not enough.
When a windy sand whips through, I feel tangled.
Full of knots.
Wrestling breathless with a rope of what is working
and what's not.

Life becomes what we call it,
earn, win...
on our own vibrant terms.

Okay then
make art.

Win the best of the best
way to be,
which is
all you can be,
that to me, has a name:
Joie de Vivre. Joie de Vivre. Joie de Vivre:
my boho art mantra.

Embrace,
and quite fully,
it all…

Part Two: de *(of)* Breaking Through

She sits
watches smoke
spiral upward
asking Camels
for creation
of a thought.
She inhales
an old moment
burns her lungs
leaving only
ashes on the glass.
Flowers lived
in the hand of
she who picked them
breathing daisies
into death's
paper vase.

Thunder Haiku

Thunder God shouts out.
Nature is smirking again.
Man—you are *so* SMALL.

Battlefield

Moving thru
feelings
dug out
trenches
and tunnels
and fox holes.
Held out
'til the war came
proclaiming
its battlefield
at my doorstep.
Quicksand's tough
to pull out of
don't leave no
footsteps
can be seen
behind nor ahead.
Carry grace
like a weapon,
invisible ally.
Wear goggles
and helmet,
a bullet-proof vest,
only follow your nose.
Move thru
fronts
ice you over.
There's sleet on
your face
mud-caked skin.

'Til the hail comes
upon you
sting gloriously—
wash hard creases
away. Hope
someday
you'll emerge
someone new.

Patchwork

I pass thru
moments
of insecurity
like cotton thread
thru the eye
of a needle
so slim
and fragile
struggling to be
on the other side
without
breaking first.

Buffalo Robe

Hollow hugs
I not warmed
by your coals
cold wind
blows ashes
red into black
bite my bones
bitter air
how I wish
you a buffalo
robe I once
wrapped myself in.

You a grand bear
would claw down
the doors to
find me
scratching symbols
you hoped
summed up true
on the door jamb
paw stuck in
a honey jar
bee stings
can kill
when allergic
reaction runs rampant.

New moon
to unfold in
full bloom
cross your arrows
from tribe to tribe
trusting the path
where red meat
bleeds red blood
wrap yourself
in a crosswind
and learn
just to trust
as with buffalo
robe I once
wrapped myself in.

Crumbs

Tonight, Crystal broke a cracker on the floor. As she tried to pick up the pieces it kept breaking. Again and again. Until all that was left was one chance for retrieving a handful of crumbs. She wanted to cry. But that seemed so pathetic. Instead, Crystal held the crumbs. And she tried to name them. Fido. Rudolph. Rocky. James Bond. You know... names like that. Names that can fight for themselves.

Lone Wolf in Three Howls

1.

Today I saw a heavy older man, working class kinda guy, bundled up and breathing hard, trying to make it across a busy South Broadway near the old Gates factory and the new Design Center.

A heavy older man, working class kinda guy, was bundled up and breathing hard, working so surely at this particular challenging moment of life – scuffling with a sad, forced energy just to make it across one lousy metropolitan street.

And I sensed, these are the kind of tough, tired, already spent moments some beings must live the construction paper chain of.

And suddenly I too was tired, oh so tired, but still wanting to *be* the paper chain *before* it was made and certainly not any mundane street of life its links might lead to.

Suddenly I was a spent man trying too hard
to hold on...

while in reality I just drove the car, the Subaru Forester, with its cozy heater humming, and I cried.

2.

Yesterday I witnessed an inflamed cop drive up onto a
median, going the wrong direction, at a congested city
intersection to run an endlessly insulting check on a
homeless vet who was ... "panhandling." I never saw how
that scenario played out, but I deplored the look on the
cop's face while he sat in his shiny protective cage of a car.
Yet I felt somehow inspired by the maimed vet, standing
quite stoic, looking into the sky, smoking a cigarette.

3.

Live
in the skin
of a lone wolf.
Track
eye of the enemy,
eye of life source,
source no other wolf sees.
Breathe up
through thick fur,
all covered in snow,
pulling shadow at dawn,
crossing thin ice alone
is survival.
Some creatures know this
sadness
gold pebble stream bed
lays out
for stream carry away.

Run

I sit, with crisp volunteer blindfold
while dignity takes a cold hit.

No blame here, right?
Each man, each woman…
respectfully, rightfully *blind*.

Especially those who would force us
to suddenly see *it* their way
while craftily stealing our money
for drummed up ill legalite.

Eyes open. Or not.
Spend a dark night in jail
if you really are craving to see.

But beware, should you choose this
floor essence,

you'll be made into hostage for:

Facing your suspect,
seeing cracked mirror,
trying to run when there's nowhere to go,
running from jailers,
running from villains,
running from Star of Another Man's Show.

Running and running and running and running,
your angst is the theme of that other man's show.

No worries, no hurries, you're cool and you're beautiful, cooler,
more beautiful, you're on, you're you.

You're fast and you're furious magic and mojo;
You know how, you know where, you know why
to go.

Run… Run… Run…
Run.

The Inconvenient Truth

Change will not wait for you to drink another beer.

Change doesn't care if Walking Dead
is streaming live.

Change won't wait for us to bail.
Or for our pirate ship to sail.
Change. Is not. Convenient.

It asks that we show up all senses open to this day.

Change hopes you know your name
in at least one honest language.
It runs like cool, cool water that is never short supply.

Change wants us to grieve necessary losses and go on.

It is angry, it is light.
It is loving, it is dark.

Equals courage, plus conviction, less conditions
times countless change agent voices... for a start.

You Are Here

Everything is a hole in the wall.
My house, your house, the kids' preschool playhouse,
your office,
the bank vault, and
Safe
deposit
box,
Church hall, vestibule, choir loft, altar...
the brothel, the prison, the penthouse...
the castle, the treehouse, the cave.

Everything is a
Hole
In
The
Wall.

You step into it/you step out of it.
You step over it/you step under it.
You step A-r-o-u-n-d...
It's always the same
Hole
In
The
Wall...
and you're stuck there, wanting it to be different
while constantly searching for home.

I grew up missing home. Drove west to find home. Sailed far to trade home for home for home.
Finding only that
each port and portal
was just another
Hole
In
The
Wall.

So I put the hole-in-the-wall of a backpack onto my hole-in-the-wall of a back and went deep into woods seeking truth. Crawled into the hole of a pup tent, sleeping bag, sleep.

A cool rain came through soon to sing me awake, these Rumi words that I heard:

"Wanderer, stay hungry, and honor your exile. Wherever we came from in the first place, that's where we're headed."

Learned to read my own palm:

If you cannot find yourself right where you are, where do you expect to find you?

You Are Here.

Runway

1.

Downing Street
February 2016

A coyote ran scared before me today and he did not seem to know where he was going. I tried to slow down in my car on a simple city street so as not to scare him. But he seemed scared nonetheless. As I got closer, I realized he was sad. Troubled. And hurt. Wounds on his skin. Skinny tail tucked. This brave coyote. In winter. In the city. Sometimes life is like that. For us all.

2.

Harper's Bazaar
March 2016

"There's something unmistakably modern about a Valentino dress. At the house's Spring couture shows… gowns floated down the runway on barefoot models with gold snakes in their hair, as though from another world. But there's nothing mythical about the making of a dress. It comes down to talent, labor, and time. How much time? Some 2,800 hours. For Firmament d'Etoiles, Valentino's powder-rose paneled dress, that is. Oiseau Psychedelique, the green velvet gown that was arguably the show's centerpiece, took 1,800 hours to craft. ... With everyone questioning what drives haute couture's soaring price tags, lifting the veil was refreshingly demystifying. This season is about evolution and progress ~ and about *breaking free* and *letting loose*. Chanel constructed a temple of serenity...where models glided down a grassy, Zen-like garden of a runway...in the legendary Le Palace with models in sequined and embroidered robes waving champagne glasses. It's not just fashion that's changing, it's the business of fashion, and the issue on everyone's mind is how to adapt."

3.

City Park
April 2016

A friend calls me in tears. "Meet me in City Park for tea," she cries. "My rent just doubled. I'm out tomorrow. Hitting the road. All the way out."

4.

A coyote runs scared before me. He does not know where to go. I slow down in my car so as not to scare him. But he is scared. Nonetheless.

The Sound of One Howl Howling

For the "Go Outside and Howl at 8pm" Movement,
helping people everywhere break through
the isolation of the Covid Pandemic.

To hear the close distance,
your howl, when unable to find
one cold sliver of moon.

I opened warm window.
This frozen stuck body of me
shifting over to what it must be
in a house made of worry
and flammable things.

When survival is one hungry beast
lighting fires fast as
bear claws unleashed
in this box of a house, any house,
to find food, any food, feed
that soul hungry beast
eating sliver of moon
cooling fire on face of a moment
of hard-assed especially sweet stuff, any life.

I listen for line to connection.

Hear hot pulse of warm blood,
surprisingly bright, bursting
through like great wolf
shedding cloak of sheep's clothing
is this, yawping call from

a place I can't see, only feel,
coming back like a boomerang self
to wild safety, close distance,
raw sound of one howl howling now.

Maintain

porcelain vase
      sits on table's edge
      peers onto
      hard splintered
      oak unyielding
      the break
      to countless fragments
      pieced together
      do avoid
         the crash

Curve of Her World

Wraps herself in a blanket of fire.
Others think she is burning
her core, it is safe.
Keeps so still 'til an itching
brings truth she now knows
after living their lies.

She, always making her bed.
She, always smoothing the wrinkled rough fabric.
She, always shaping the curve of her world.

It whirls round her then stops.
Like a top spun all out.

One by one she is laying clay bricks,
making home, where she finds herself
aching and longing for more of what's not
with her now.

To her, fighting fair begins with a battle that
rages within.
She's alone, climbing big steps: three forward,
two back.
Laughing through tears, she gets lost in a sea
of emotion.
Romantic red tape.

Is it true they all know her much better than she
knows herself?
Crystal guide. Lead the way. Through these blankets
of fire.
Not burning her core. Shape the curve of her world.

Fear Races On

I am the deer being hunted,
you are the man with a gun.
I am the food on your table
and getting ready to run.

    I am the deer being hunted,
    you are the man with a gun.
    I am the food on your table
    and getting ready to run.

        He is the deer being hunted,
        she is the man with a gun.
        We are the food on the table,
        let's all get ready to run, run...

            Running,
            fear races on
            tormented
            the gut screams
            ferocious
            in anguish
            an echo
            speaks softly
            while dangling
            the face bruised
            shines back
            mirrored portrait
            to hear

healing cry
as the wounded
come forth
take back breath
lost while
running, running, running...
fear races on.

We are the deer being hunted.

Scrubbing the Karma Out of My Skin

Scrubbing the karma out of my skin
trust means to be free
though tears fall from my skies
threat of cloud fronts explode in my ears
wind-whipped, storm-kicked,
throat-choked blood
turns clear to snow white,
tears, more tears,
salt-stained eyes of stone maiden.

Whole scrapbooks fall out as old pieces of life
fly about
little outbursts these bits of sheer bad
unexpectedly surface to
fall apart, come loose, break free–
allow me scrub dead dark
of ancient stuff off.

What are these rough things stuck hard to soft skin
like so many black barnacles, clinging,
as if they belonged to this ship?

Please stop me from telling that story now.

Time this began
become cold fire,
cremation pyre,
debt already paid
at high price.

Smell of reckless gone mad as burnt rubber on asphalt.
Not born yet, thrown under fast tires just the same...

Trust means to be free.
Let that story end.
Scrub Karma out of my skin.

Dream On

the last broken dream
fractures slowly
while eyes
are still coated with sleep
somnambulant
sleepwalker
gropes in the darkness
takes mindful
of moments
not lived yet
for blind strolls
'round corners
edge further
from archway
to kitchen
won't feed it no more

sleepwalker
brings armload
of pieces of dream
stumbles through
a screened doorway
to compost pile
heap of sighs
slip now
through moonlight
one cracked gem
of hope
for this
tired
charade

escapes
to a starflight
all gone
tarnished vision
moves on
out of reach

sleepwalker is driven
no, pulled
by mysterious force
some call dreamtime
is whispering
garden... your garden
new seed
plant new seed
with your eyes closed
till soil
wake up
to a waterfall
gently on
field of dream
amethyst, rose quartz
wake up
to a crystal
to know it
so clearly
is yours
clearly real
crystal clear
anew
dream will come
sleepwalker
dream on

Love Poem #1 (to love)

Oh love.

I would have held your hand
no matter what.

You filled my heart
with paper scraps,
candles lit. And burned.

Words on starlight drifting.
Smiles through fun house mirror.
Torn Bits of Every, Single, Thing.

You Filled my heart
with rebel bliss, untangled knots.

Blowing kisses, softly landing. There.
You told me I am beauty. I believed you.

Oh love.

I would have kissed your lips
no matter what.

Centuries of OCD

Angel visited
every cemetery
west
of the Mississippi
before
she could go
home.

Wild Silence

Too much noise
penetrates
brings unwilling to speak
as in way that one
stutters and stammers
and mumbles near mute
in a world of too many loud words
none belonging to
this child
this child
this child
of chaos confusion pain crises
and love.

Sad lump in throat chakra;
what seems like great silence is not.

Tense murmur of see listen feel
such an
overwhelm
overwhelm
overwhelm
one cannot speak.

Understand then that *no speak* may not always mean
quietly.

Wild silence
is chaos confusion pain crises
too many loud words

none belonging to
this child
this child
this sad silent child
of love.

too mundane

Demands of the day
split you in half
while the toast burns brown/black
pat of butter melts into oblivion.

You wish for one thick
slice of purple to eat so this
life will not taste too mundane.

Cold Plunge

Who is this woman
I rise out of sleep
with today swirl of
3am strangeness
is threatening
to wake her
forever
with plunge
of cold madness
cannot be ignored
anymore as
fleece pullover catches
warm tears telling
stories again but the
cuckoo clock broke long ago
and the night owl has forever flown
while the mockingbird calls in her head
from sad place she must leave now.

Rush of cold plunge gives way
to fast swim in fresh lake
of surrender where sad stories
dissolve like a school
of translucent gold fish
that was only alive in her mind
disappear and be forever gone.

There's a new moon approaching.

Red Moon Haiku

moonrise east red red
when it waxes white once more
this girl will be changed

Part Three: Vivre *(Life)*
Breaking Free

Sky
speaks
volumes.
Rain
sky
rain.

Your Ocean

Written on December 13, 1993
for my mother, Aline Vezina

I went to the ocean
and there I found you,
your spirit, a wave
rolling
grief bank
swept over me
dancing and prancing
on sand
singing song of
abandoned one.
I know that you
never hoped to leave
us motherless
all your children
continue to grieve
loss of you
French Canadian woman
who journeyed
away from her
native ground
found mate
some fifty-odd years
and a soul song ago.

People say you died young
but for you
life was old

old as I always
knew you to be
never young
to the ninth child
could see
what a big price you paid
for eleven of us that you fed
bathed and nursed
through long nights
of our childhood illnesses
nightmares.

I always felt special
when sickness
befell me
because you were
not only
mother but nurse
who'd left lovely Quebec
for the US Midwest
where you put
care you could
into home.

I'm still nursing the wound
that your death
gave to me,
sometimes pour from it
buckets of tears like soft
rainwater falling
in gray sheets to cleanse.
Every year early on in December
I turn a blue hue

while the sad
seventeen-year-old
girl in me
cries out
for mother she lost
in the night twenty years
from this day
counting back
through all Christmases
we knew without you.

Count back
past the times
you weren't there
to the times that you were
making sure
Santa Claus came
though mostly on wish and a prayer
on a shoestring
he came bringing
mythical sleighful of
gifts wrapped in love
of your offspring
an oversized brood
that sang out
the French carols you taught us
tradition you loved
and passed on
like the Réveillon
midnight feast following
Catholic mass Christmas Eve
something you brought
from the province

you never forgot
like the wedding vows
seen in a band of gold worn
many years, counting back
seasons, your life
held strong bonds
did not lose their strength
when the times held
confusion and chaos
or poverty crosses to bear.

Joie de Vivre was there
underneath all your worries
your birthright shown through
like the desert rose
short-lived but packed
with such beauty
your smile
and laughter so charged
with a spirit for life
that you passed on
to us
one by one
each by each
from the sidelines
of chronic depression
that weight on your back
not too heavy
for coaching your kids:
find the way
set your sight
field your dreams.
And believe you we did

you believed every
one of us
carried your birthright
so right you were
still are
in memories
vivid
roll forward
like waves
counting back
to the lifetime
we saw as
your ocean.

Same ocean
that mothers me now
brought me conch shell
in shape of a female
torso to honor
the day
when I'd journeyed
from US Midwest
to West Indian seaside
and found you
Aline Vezina
found your ocean
your spirit, a wave.

Poem for Joseph

Big brother
the laughing piano man
gave up Muscatel nights
to become GI Joe.

Forever he carried
one gift,
the Big Heart.

Cinderella, I was
for he, the prince
had multiple plans
to make slippers fit
shaping feet
through kind ways
to warm glass.

From paper route rustler
to super boy sacker
this hootenanny king proved
young men
run on drive.

Courage pilot
was made flying Cross
shrouded in nightmare's cape
to watch Vietnam
disappear
into Ambition Mountains
made magic
that safe piano bench.

While with beauty
his women
did balance one end
little sister
would ponder the other.

Butcher paper banner
read "Welcome Home Joe,"
always a heart prayed return
in ivory the keys
of his soul.

Oasis of You

for my siblings

Your love keeps me
beautifully safe.
Like a savvy & spirited
star that shines
brightly on open
horizons. While
crossing all shores
to full life,
this sister is drawn
to Oasis of You.

Moon Shine

Moon shines so full I fear
it may explode white nothingness
to obliterate illusions
that I tell myself I am.

While reading of this day warns
it's important not collapse
into illusory emotions
at the center of myself.

I think
of every love
I've held so close
it truly was
as if the moon
itself I'd held
as if the moon
itself had melted
into warmest
heart on fire.

As if the moon's white
glow alone could shatter
every bit of darkness
spinning open spinning sharply
into fractals of a thing.

I'd never hold, instead let go.
To be released
as this wild human

ever being fully lit
with moon on fire's
bright white glow.
      the energy of
        nothingness~
So fully full I need not fear...
so fully full we need not fear...

So fully full
there is
no fear.

Cupid

Do not send love notes if you cannot love...
she wrote.
Don't ask what's love if you can't hear what is...
he wrote.
And so they tangoed up 'n down them walls.

Cupid
was confused.

Ode to Poetry

Poetry is a lucid dream to save us from the dark.

It's every lover
known
drawing blood-red
ink-stained maps
'cross all these pages
of a heart.

The first great love of mine, that never went away,
is with Poetry...
It's the one whose signature I kept.

Poetry wakes me at midnight and tells me "never go back
to sleep" then wakes me again at 3am, asking where I've
been. Sounds off a few hours later like a wet dog barking
to get out of the rain. I arise, suddenly resigned to the
discomforts of a poetic fall, knowing afterall, I will drink
my tea with vodka-splashed words while looking thru the
ether leaves at *a life called Poesie.*

But really, Poesie is my milk and my honey ~ of course ~
but it's also a mad virus I caught long ago. It tears me to
pieces and then screws me together again. Poetry: Solder
my lines to my spine, not in order, confuse me with
kisses... while clearing my head. Make me want to reach
high high, the way that my soul tells me to. Send me a
Valentine message of script sealed in blood, dropped from
beak of a heretofore lost carrier pigeon.

Proclaim This !

TODAY
poetry blew
all my fuses,
and then started a fire
in the house of me
until all that was left is
pure ash with no thing
to contain it, pure ash such as
I never knew could be *so* beautiful.

First Snow

When the first snow falls
Hush like a slumbering child
Cold that cannot hurt
Feeling sleep will never end.

I am a candle on the sill
A steamy pane of glass reflecting
Fallen stars back to their sky.

In a cool white silence
I can hear the beating heart
of all that is all that is.

For Sarah

Jack stood at the corner of Hollywood and Vine having
coffee with his ex. But this was not the usual kind of coffee
visit. As he poured a stream of liquid dark roast onto the
pavement and watched it roll into the curbside grating, a
beautiful wispy steam appeared. Jack loved this. What he
thought of as the energy of Sarah. And it made him happy
every day for a month now that any drunken idiot could
murder the body of a person, but no one can kill the
energy of human spirit.

Solstice Poem

When light surrounds darkness
we see where we are
we know how to carry out journey
of bright love
of this love
of our love
so sun filled and star lit
and so so so so
overflowing
with yes yes yes yes
to Infinity.

We
see/hear/feel our way
us together
in laughter and quieter sounds
of quite serious things we must now find/explore
in order to make sense of darkness
surrounded by light
in order to fully know meaning of light
as it shines through all important places we share.

Dreams are a fine place to be
when the light finds the darkness
dream me/I'll dream you
and we'll wake to such splendid sensations
in real time
again.

Found Art

To spot a diamond bit
among crushed beer cans
and rusty cars
is to find truth
in this man-made world.

Strangely Naked

1.

I just could not imagine that I would ever *cut my hair.*
Flowing, healthy, Rapunzelish…long.

"Like silk and honey," my lover would say as he brushed
it for me in the morning sunlight that spun off the edge of
our bed. Oh yes, people remarked often at an
unquestionable beauty of the hair that had grown itself
into my center of my identity. Oh yes, I wore that hair with
a dangerous pride. "Would be a sin if you ever cut it," a
strange man once said as I stood, aloof, daydreaming, in a
grocery store line. It took me a moment to realize he was
talking to me. I smiled shyly, never sure how to respond to
these comments while loving them too much. And yes,
there were days I actually believed *I was* my hair.

2.

*The house smelled of burnt hair. But the woman was dancing
and she did not care. Not like she had moments earlier when
despair had seemed to cripple her with a feeling of blinders and
bullets at once. She had thought this would kill her. She had
thought she was dying. Burning. To death. It was only her hair.
While she pitied herself cold, wishing only to be warm, she'd
crouched down before gas flame feeling sorry for herself as her
fine hair began to catch fire. It smoldered and smoked. Charred
and ashen. It split off in small handfuls of uneven streamers all
strewn about the studio floor. The horror had been hers alone.
Now, minutes later, she danced.*

3.

I buried my hair like a dead pet, the ashes of an old friend, at the base of an Evergreen tree. They say we hold memory in hair. Once I realized what was stored in that 18-inch-long and very thick swatch of silk and honey, I felt oddly happy to just let it go. And strangely naked for months. I wasn't exactly bald. Hair still draped my shoulders. It was just that so much was gone. Strangely naked, I began to forget what I look like often. Strangely naked, I began to *see* more. Laughter, movement, color. Graceful, flowing, essence. Strangely naked. I began to *be. More.*

Hair Extension

I grow my hair
I cut my hair
I wash my hair
I blow it clean.
I grow my hair
I cut my hair
I'm not my hair
And it's not me.
I wash my face
I paint my face
I paint my face
I scrub it clean.
I grow my hair
I cut my hair
I'm not my hair
And it's not me.
I wash my hands
I dirty them
I'm not my hands
And they're not me.
I paint my face
I'm not my face
I grow my hair
But it's not me.
I'm not my hair
I'm not my hair
I'm not *my hair*…
I'm energy.

Bad Dog Days

A team of men with chainsaws is taking down another tree in my hood. There's a gaping hole to the sky where a canopy was. The sun is dumping heat waves of an angry sort of *told ya so* onto every brick house it can reach. But I love the sun, and the sun knows I love it. So it blows me a kiss, then burns me again. Just to remind me who's boss.

Electric Blue Sky Above Sky

Ether: upper regions of air beyond clouds.
Ether: celestial energy filling all space.
Ether: a place we sense deeply yet can never touch.

Ether:
radically cosmic,
plugged in electric blue,
sky above sky.

One day I shall marry my bones to the dirt
and my soul to an ether-bound height.
Such a megawatt wise air
won't care if I find it in shadows of tree grove
or play of sun rays
always dancing 'round tan sand,
black mud, or bright snow.

Ether will find me
whenever it finds in me,
shape to be opened, old vessel split free.

Into ether I fly with my feet on the ground.
I am crystal and pearl, dirt and clay,
dark translucence alive
in a body of things I am learning to know. Differently.

With eyes closed to old habit of being I see:
I have not understood that my name is invisible wisdom
we're born with.

This I will answer to once I have fully accepted my one
true birth place.

Once I've grasped namelessness I was born with,
I will become one that knows how to hold *now*,
unclutchably tight, onto nothing.

Electric blue, wild, undeniable elusive essence.
Of nothing.

Then
my name will be marked
with invisible seal
on the frame of my real home,
one with no structure at all.

The Truth of a Good Fairy Tale

In reality
Cinderella lost
the glass slipper
but won a true prize.
His name was Rugged,
and he drove an old
Chevy 4x4 pickup
that provided
a sure-thing
denim ride
to forever.

The Sky of Us

for Tom

1.
There. A day. I first saw you.
Such solid stature at such a young age.
And a heart full of kindness.
I saw you stand powerfully quiet
as a young tree in one calm split second.
With eyes full of sky.
You were looking my way.
Words not easy back then.
Could not speak. So terribly shy.
Shy as me, shy as you.
I felt something instead.
Reaching out from split second of moment,
as if you were handing me
piece of soft sky
before it could turn hard again.

2.
Many hundreds and thousands of days
would then carry the unspoken distance between us.
The lump in my throat softened now.
I can open my mouth, feel pure words
like blue butterflies fly freely out.
To remember. Was you that once offered
me glimpse of a sky that is us.
I speak now. But there's too much to say.
Instead kisses are calling us
into deep gaze of pure knowing
soft bright to be shared.

3.
And I
want to kiss you
clear up to the sky of us
bluest of blue beyond clouds, so high high.
Strong wind blows through what feels
like strong branches
two trees that we are, full
of vibrant leaves, starlings, ripe fruit.
With the clearest of eyes
we can see all the way to forever.
Split second. That moment. This gaze. Tender us.
My skin longs for your touch. That began.
On a day. I first saw you, appear in split second,
shy boy, there you were, reaching out of soft gaze,
to this girl as if sharing gold key, endless sky.

Poetry of Now

Sometimes you must wait for the house to go to sleep.
There are nights when the street must take a silent stand
as well.
And the dog would rather dream of quiet bone than chew
out loud…

In the vacuum of…
The silence of…
The narrow space…
The hall…

Lies an empty silver staircase
to the Poetry of Now.

Rooms full of nothing more
than weightless words pouring out.
Stairwells leading to clear open
beckon you to write it all.

Do not run and do not rest.
Do not crawl back to bed.
Let black ink flow, white keys dance,
words tumble from your head.

House will sleep, dog will dream.
Poetry will right you now.

Love Poem #2 (to poetry)

This one love poem. Licks you. Passionately.
Everywhere. Always.
This one love poem. Is willing to walk into a
dark room. With you.
This one love poem. Is wearing nothing.
In the light of everything.

This one love poem.
Wants you more than you want yourself.

It is here. This love. In a poem at the center of a well
you will fall into.
Whether you want to or not. But you will fall nonetheless.
Willingly.

This is the poem you wrote the day you were born.
This is the poem you said you would never say.
This is the poem that talks through the mouth.
Of your soul.

You tie your shoes. And try to walk. Knowing that without this
one love. Poem.

There is nowhere to go.

Acknowledgements

Poems in this collection, previously published, are:

"Smoking Poet"
Faces

"Poem for Joseph," and "Crisis"
Rocky Mountain Arsenal of the Arts

"Patchwork"
Tangents VI
Thalia Anthology (Mile High Poetry)

"Lone Wolf"
Mad Blood #1

"Found Art,"; "Thunder Haiku,"; "For Sarah"
Lummox

"Eldorado Night Sky,"; "Wild Silence,";
"Strangely Naked"
Semicolon

"Your Ocean"
My Mother, Myself (River Sanctuary Publishing)

"Thunder Haiku," "Mountain Writing Itself," and "Electric
Blue Sky Above Sky"
Love Shovel Review

"Runway"
Punch Drunk Poetry Anthology

"Crumbs"
Punch Drunk Press Online Journal

"The Sound of One Howl Howling"
Covid-19 Manuscript Collection
(History Colorado Permanent Archives)
and *Thought for Food Anthology*
(South Broadway Press)

"Colorado Woman Song"
They

"Ode to Poetry," and "Writer's Block"
Solid Mercury

About the Author

Roseanna Frechette is in love with words. Written, spoken, published, or not. It's all about words on the page and energy on stage. Longtime member of Denver's thriving poetry community, and former publisher of Rosebud Forum *magazine*, Roseanna holds great passion for the bohemian underground and all things alternative / independent when it comes to art. Dancer and yogi, as well as multi-genre writer and performance poet, she has equal respect for pure beauty of nature, and edgy intrigue of urban culture. Her "First Collection: 13 Poems" was released in '91. Since then, writings of Roseanna's have appeared on many pages, like so many etchings on leaves to be scattered to the wind. Her work has featured on public TV and radio as well as festival stages including Arise, Boulder Fringe, and Colorado Poetry Rodeo. She is the reigning Dead Poets Slam Champion for her portrayal of Anaïs Nin. Named one of Westword's "100 Colorado Creatives," Roseanna tends to create from whatever ground she happens to be standing on.

En Avant
(Onward)

www.ingramcontent.com/pod-product-compliance
Lightning Source LLC
Chambersburg PA
CBHW021240090426
42740CB00006B/625